HANDMADE PHOTO ALBUMS

COMPLETE INSTRUCTIONS FOR MAKING 18 FUN AND CREATIVE DESIGNS

Creative Publishing
international

First published in 2007 by
Creative Publishing international, Inc.
18705 Lake Drive East
Chanhassen, Minnesota 55317
1-800-328-3895
www.creativepub.com
All rights reserved

President/CEO: Ken Fund
VP Sales & Marketing: Peter Ackroyd
Executive Managing Editor: Barbara Harold
Creative Director: Michele Lanci-Altomare
Production Managers: Laura Hokkannen, Linda Halls
Design Manager: Jon Simpson
Design: Eddie Goldfine
Editor: Shoshana Brickman
Layout: Gala Pre Press Ltd.

Copyright 2007 Penn Publishing Ltd.

Printed in China
10 9 8 7 6 5 4 3 2 1

Library of Congress Cataloging-in-Publication Data

Porath, Tami.
  Handmade photo albums : complete instructions for making 18 fun and
creative designs / Tami Porath.
      p. cm.
Includes index.
  ISBN-13: 978-1-58923-347-8 (soft cover)
  ISBN-10: 1-58923-347-6 (soft cover)
  1. Photograph albums. 2. Photographs--Conservation and restoration.
3. Scrapbooks. I. Title.

TR465.P65 2007
745.593--dc22   2007010508

HANDMADE PHOTO ALBUMS

COMPLETE INSTRUCTIONS FOR MAKING 18 FUN AND CREATIVE DESIGNS

By

TAMI PORATH

Creative Publishing
international

Contents

Introduction

My life has always been bound by photography. Photographs, paper memories, cameras, and albums. As a child, I worked with my father in his dark room, developing black and white photographs, watching images appear is if by magic on the paper. I eventually became a professional photographer, taking photographs for movies, advertisements, fashion, and architecture.

I often worked as part of a large team, on movie sets or on location, with or without actors or models. My technical background and familiarity with the finer points of shading and lighting allowed me to achieve excellent results. However, it was the relationships with the people on the other side of the lens that was the real charm of my work.

When I became a mother, I wanted to spend more time at home and less time on location. I found a distinct pleasure in studio and event photography. Whether I was photographing portraits in my studio or elegant events at large halls, it was the connection with individuals that was most fulfilling. What a thrill to be part of people's most special events, and be instrumental in preserving the memories.

Creating personalized albums to house these photographs was a natural extension of my work. Clients wanted something to preserve these important memories, and I delighted in the chance to meet this need by combining papers, textiles, and leathers in colorful and distinct ways that harmonized with the events themselves and provided permanent homes for these photographs. This led me to learn bookbinding, an ancient craft of precision, skill, and beauty.

In the following pages, I'm delighted to share with you the techniques I have learned for building personalized photograph albums. The process is unhurried and soothing, beautiful and rewarding. It requires time and precision, as well as creativity and imagination. It is a process that improves over time, as one gains familiarity with the materials, and experience with the techniques.

About the Author

Tami Porath has been taking pictures all of her life. She has photographed everything from scripted movies to family affairs, from staged events to the most spontaneous moments. Tami's deep connection with the people she photographs naturally branched into a line of distinctive albums. Diverse and distinct, these albums combine timeless techniques with a modern sense of style and remarkable personal touches.

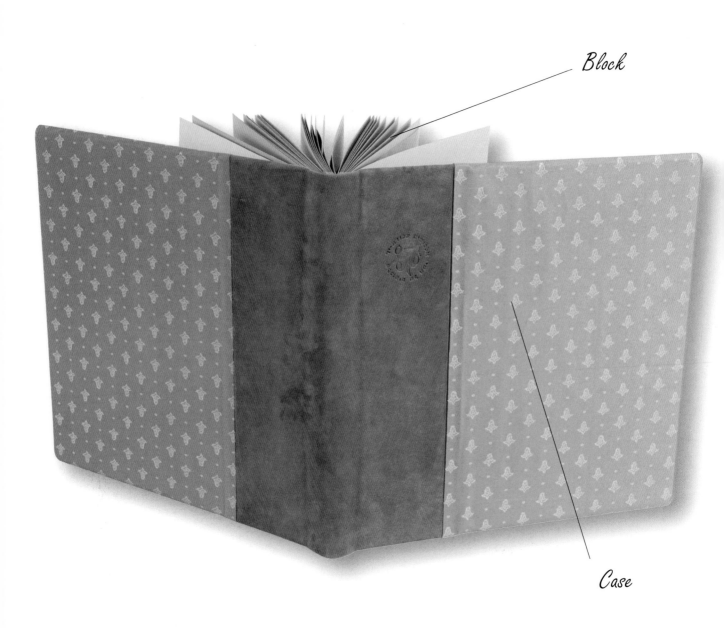

Block

Case

Back endpaper

Interleaves

Rounded corner

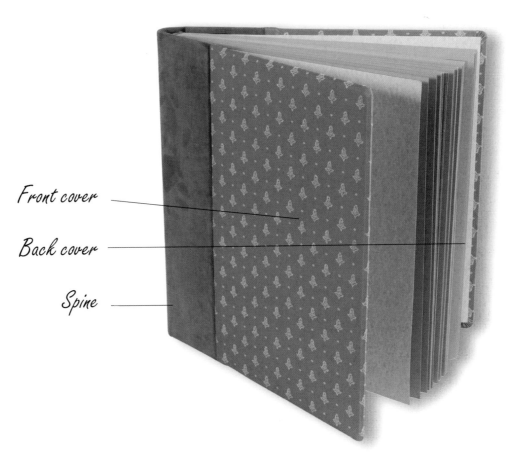

Front cover

Back cover

Spine

Types of Albums

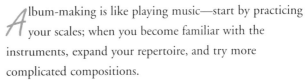

*A*lbum-making is like playing music—start by practicing your scales; when you become familiar with the instruments, expand your repertoire, and try more complicated compositions.

In the following pages, you'll read detailed descriptions of how to make albums for a variety of occasions. Each album is accompanied by a table with dimensions for every aspect of its construction, and creative suggestions on choosing materials and arranging the photographs. Basic steps for building the albums are described on pages 58 to 103. Adapt the size of the materials according to the album you choose.

Wedding Album

Bridal Couple

40 PAGES, 13³/₄" X 13¹/₂" (34.9CM X 34.2CM)

The perfect album for a couple's perfect day

This is the album of a lifetime—a collection of memories from a couple's most special day. The size of this album is quite large, easily accommodating at least 330 photographs.

- Be sure to use the best materials you can find for this album, as you want it to be as beautiful after fifty years of marriage as it is on your first anniversary.
- Take photographs of important pre-event preparations, such as choosing rings and dress fittings. These make a lovely first chapter in the book.
- Think of the wedding colors when choosing the fabric. You'll want to use colors that evoke the event—you may even want to use the same material that was chosen for the tablecloths or bridal canopy.
- Print or handwrite lyrics of the Wedding Song onto an interleaf.
- Arrange the photographs according to themes such as Ceremony, Reception, Dancing, and Around the Tables.
- Glue three sides of a piece of paper to the endpaper at the back of the album to make an envelope for storing a DVD of the affair.

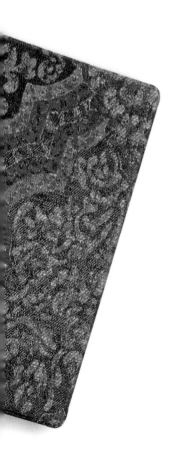

FINAL SIZE		13 ³/₄" x 13 ¹/₂"	**(34.9cm x 34.2cm)**
FOLD		³/₄"	**(2cm)**
PAPER WEIGHT		**80 lb**	**(215 gsm)**

BLOCK

Papers	40	14" x 13"	(35.6cm x 33cm)
Interleaves	39	12 ¹/₄" x 12 ¹/₂"	(31.1cm x 31.8cm)
Endpapers	2	26 ³/₄" x 13"	(67.9cm x 33cm)
Light cotton fabric	1	2 ³/₄" x 12 ¹/₄"	(7cm x 31.1cm)

CASE

Binder's boards	2	13 ³/₈" x 13 ³/₄"	(33.9cm x 35cm)
Lightweight board	1	10 ⁵/₈" x 13 ³/₄"	(27cm x 35cm)
Binder's boards	2	6 ¹/₄" x 13 ³/₈"	(22cm x 33.9cm)
Binder's boards	2	3 ³/₄" x 13 ³/₈"	(9.5cm x 33.9cm)
Leather	1	11 ⁵/₈" x 15 ³/₈"	(29.5cm x 39cm)
Book cloth	1	11" x 15 ³/₈"	(27.9cm x 39cm)

Wedding Album

Parents of the Bride / Parents of the Groom

40 PAGES, 10¼" X 10¼" (26CM X 26CM)

A special gift for parents of the new couple
This album should be smaller than the bridal couple's album, as it only includes guests from one side of the wedding. At the same time, it should be large enough to include lots of family photographs and collages.

- If there are photographs with people who won't be recognized by this side of the family, cut out the irrelevant faces and arrange the familiar one in a collage.
- Take the wedding colors into consideration when choosing the fabric and the paper. You may even want to use colors similar to the dress worn by the mother of the bride or mother of the groom.
- Print or handwrite a special message from the bride and groom onto an interleaf.

FINAL SIZE		10 $^1/_4$" x 10 $^1/_4$"	(26cm x 26cm)
FOLD		$^3/_4$"	(2cm)
PAPER WEIGHT		80 lb	(215 gsm)

BLOCK

Papers	40	10 $^7/_8$" x 9 $^7/_8$"	(27.6cm x 25.1cm)
Interleaves	39	9 $^1/_2$" x 9 $^1/_2$"	(24.1cm x 24.1cm)
Endpapers	2	19 $^5/_8$" x 9 $^7/_8$"	(49.8cm x 25.1cm)
Light cotton fabric	1	2 $^3/_4$" x 9"	(7cm x 22.8cm)

CASE

Binder's boards	2	10" x 10 $^1/_4$"	(25.5cm x 26cm)
Lightweight board	1	9 $^1/_4$" x 10 $^1/_4$"	(23.5cm x 26cm)
Binder's boards	2	6" x 10"	(15.2cm x 25.5cm)
Binder's boards	2	3 $^3/_8$" x 10"	(8.6cm x 25.5cm)
Leather	1	10 $^1/_4$" x 11 $^7/_8$"	(26cm x 30.1cm)
Book cloth	1	7 $^7/_8$" x 11 $^7/_8$"	(20cm x 30.1cm)

Wedding Anniversary

40 PAGES, 13³/₄" X 13¹/₂" (34.9CM X 34.2CM)

Commemorating a lifetime of memories together

Is there any better way to celebrate parents' (or grandparents') anniversaries than with a beautiful album of their years together? This album should be large enough to accommodate photographs from every major life event. It can also include personal greetings from family members and close friends.

- Arrange the photographs in chronological order, starting with photographs from the couple's own wedding. If necessary, have these photographs professionally restored.
- Integrate photographs taken specifically for this album, such as photographs of children, grandchildren, or really good friends.
- Print or handwrite song lyrics, poems, or a famous family story onto the interleaves.

FINAL SIZE	13 3/4" x 13 1/2"	(34.9cm x 34.2cm)
FOLD	3/4" (2cm)	
PAPER WEIGHT	80 lb (215 gsm)	

BLOCK

Papers	40	14" x 13"	(35.6cm x 33cm)
Interleaves	39	12 1/4" x 12 1/2"	(31.1cm x 31.8cm)
Endpapers	2	26 3/4" x 13"	(67.9cm x 33cm)
Light cotton fabric	1	2 3/4" x 12 1/4"	(7cm x 31.1cm)

CASE

Binder's boards	2	13 3/8" x 13 3/4"	(33.9cm x 35cm)
Lightweight board	1	10 5/8" x 13 3/4"	(27cm x 35cm)
Binder's boards	2	6 1/4" x 13 3/8"	(22cm x 33.9cm)
Binder's boards	2	3 3/4" x 13 3/8"	(9.5cm x 33.9cm)
Leather	1	11 5/8" x 15 3/8"	(29.5cm x 39cm)
Book cloth	1	11" x 15 3/8"	(27.9cm x 39cm)

Friendship Anniversary

30 PAGES, 9^1/$_2$" X 6^7/$_8$" (24.1CM X 17.5CM)

Because best friends deserve nothing less than the best

Has it been twenty-five years since you met at the sandbox in nursery school—or thirty? When you've known someone forever (or so it seems), a photograph album recalling your years of friendship can be a walk down memory lane. Preparing this album is also a great excuse for getting in touch with old friends!

- Arrange the photographs in chronological order, starting with the first year of your friendship. Include school photographs as well—you may have to contact your friend's parents to get your hands on these!
- Include images from shared experiences, such as favorite CD covers or movie advertisements.
- Print or handwrite song lyrics, funny stories, or other shared memories onto the interleaves.

The Fifties

FINAL SIZE		9 $^1\!/_2$" x 6 $^7\!/_8$"	(24.1cm x 17.5cm)
FOLD		$^5\!/_8$" (1.6cm)	
PAPER WEIGHT		80 lb (215 gsm)	

BLOCK			
Papers	30	9 $^7\!/_8$" x 6 $^3\!/_8$"	(25.1cm x 16.2cm)
Interleaves	29	8 $^5\!/_8$" x 6 $^1\!/_8$"	(21.9cm x 15.6cm)
Endpapers	2	1 $^1\!/_8$" x 6 $^3\!/_8$"	(46cm x 16.2cm)
Light cotton fabric	1	5 $^7\!/_8$" x 2 $^1\!/_2$"	(6.4cm x 14.9cm)

CASE			
Binder's boards	2	5 $^1\!/_2$" x 6 $^7\!/_8$"	(23cm x 17.5cm)
Lightweight board	1	5 $^1\!/_2$" x 6 $^7\!/_8$"	(19.5cm x 17.5cm)
Binder's boards	2	3 $^1\!/_8$" x 6 $^3\!/_4$"	(14cm x 17cm)
Binder's boards	2	2 $^3\!/_4$" x 6 $^3\!/_4$"	(7cm x 17cm)
Leather	1	6 $^1\!/_4$" x 9"	(22cm x 21cm)
Book cloth	1	4 $^3\!/_4$" x 9 $^1\!/_2$"	(19.5cm x 21cm)

Pregnancy Album

40 PAGES, $10^{1}/4$" X $10^{1}/4$" (26CM X 26CM)

Months of anticipation; a lifetime of joy

The nine months before a baby is born are full of
anticipation, excitement, happiness, and awe. Having
photographic memories from this special period is a
wonderful way of evoking memories of those precious months
long after the baby has been born.

- Include photographs of various people, including
  the father, siblings, and grandparents, with the
  expectant mother.
- Integrate ultrasound images of the baby, and any other
  visual pre-natal information.
- Take a series of photographs in a similar pose during every
  month of the pregnancy. These photographs can make a
  wonderful collage, or serve as markers in the chronological
  progression of the album.

FINAL SIZE		10 $\frac{1}{4}$" x 10 $\frac{1}{4}$"	**(26cm x 26cm)**
FOLD		$\frac{3}{4}$" **(2cm)**	
PAPER WEIGHT		**80 lb** **(215 gsm)**	

BLOCK

Papers	40	10 $\frac{7}{8}$" x 9 $\frac{7}{8}$"	(27.6cm x 25.1cm)
Interleaves	39	9 $\frac{1}{2}$" x 9 $\frac{1}{2}$"	(24.1cm x 24.1cm)
Endpapers	2	19 $\frac{5}{8}$" x 9 $\frac{7}{8}$"	(49.8cm x 25.1cm)
Light cotton fabric	1	2 $\frac{3}{4}$" x 9"	(7cm x 22.8cm)

CASE

Binder's boards	2	10" x 10 $\frac{1}{4}$"	(25.5cm x 26cm)
Lightweight board	1	9 $\frac{1}{4}$" x 10 $\frac{1}{4}$"	(23.5cm x 26cm)
Binder's boards	2	6" x 10"	(15.2cm x 25.5cm)
Binder's boards	2	3 $\frac{3}{8}$" x 10"	(8.6cm x 25.5cm)
Leather	1	10 $\frac{1}{4}$" x 11 $\frac{7}{8}$"	(26cm x 30.1cm)
Book cloth	1	7 $\frac{7}{8}$" x 11 $\frac{7}{8}$"	(20cm x 30.1cm)

Baby Album

30 PAGES, $16\frac{1}{8}$" X $11\frac{7}{8}$" (41CM X 30.2CM)

Preserving memories of those first precious months

These are among the most cherished albums on a family bookshelf. Making one for your own baby (or for the baby of someone you care about) is a true labor of love. It may include everything from first photographs to first locks of trimmed hair. It may also include written descriptions of favorite foods and activities.

- Use fabric that is playful and youthful—if possible, choose a fabric that is similar (or identical) to the baby's favorite blanket, or something used to decorate the baby's room.
- Arrange the photographs in chronological order, but don't be afraid to stray. For example, a selection of bath photographs from a baby's first year in a collage.
- Take a series of photographs over time in which the baby is positioned beside a favorite toy. Arrange the series in a collage, or intersperse through the book, to show the baby's growth.
- Print or handwrite text—around the photographs or on the interleaves—to tell the stories behind the photographs. This may include a few sentences about adorable habits, names of good friends, and favorite funny faces.
- Glue three sides of a small piece of paper to the endpaper on the top of the album to make an envelope for storing the baby's first trimmed lock of hair.

FINAL SIZE	16 $\frac{1}{8}$" x 11 $\frac{7}{8}$"	(41cm x 30.2cm)
FOLD	$\frac{3}{4}$" (2cm)	
PAPER WEIGHT	80 lb (215 gsm)	

BLOCK

Papers	30	16 $\frac{1}{2}$" x 11"	(41.9cm x 27.9cm)
Interleaves	29	15" x 10 $\frac{5}{8}$"	(38.1cm x 27cm)
Endpapers	2	31 $\frac{1}{2}$" x 11"	(80cm x 27.9cm)
Light cotton fabric	1	2 $\frac{3}{4}$" x 9 $\frac{1}{4}$"	(7cm x 23.5cm)

CASE

Binder's boards	2	15 $\frac{3}{4}$" x 11 $\frac{3}{4}$"	(40cm x 29.8cm)
Lightweight board	1	6 $\frac{3}{4}$" x 11 $\frac{3}{4}$"	(17.1cm x 29.8cm)
Binder's boards	2	11 $\frac{3}{8}$" x 11"	(28.9cm x 27.9cm)
Book cloth	1	35 $\frac{7}{8}$" x 13 $\frac{5}{8}$"	(91.1cm x 34cm)

Family Album

40 PAGES, 13³/₄" X 13¹/₂" (34.9CM X 34.2CM)

From holidays to everydays

This album should be large and impressive, as there is no limit to the types of photographs it can include. You'll probably have hundreds of photographs to go into this album, so write out a list of themes in advance, and don't be afraid to leave out some photographs.

- Use a really special fabric to bind this album. It may even be a material taken from a family heirloom—sheets that were part of your great-grandmother's trousseau, or curtains that hung in your grandmother's living room.
- Remember that this album will probably be passed down to your grandchildren (and your great-grandchildren) so use a fabric that is classic, rather than modern.
- Take advantage of double-page spreads to tell stories, or bring together photographs relating to a similar subject.
- Include photographs from holidays, family trips, and special occasions as well as every day events, such as suppertime.

FINAL SIZE		**13 ³/4" x 13 ¹/2"**	**(34.9cm x 34.2cm)**
FOLD		³/4" (2cm)	
PAPER WEIGHT		80 lb (215 gsm)	

BLOCK

Papers	40	14" x 13"	(35.6cm x 33cm)
Interleaves	39	12 ¹/4" x 12 ¹/2"	(31.1cm x 31.8cm)
Endpapers	2	26 ³/4" x 13"	(67.9cm x 33cm)
Light cotton fabric	1	2 ³/4" x 12 ¹/4"	(7cm x 31.1cm)

CASE

Binder's boards	2	13 ³/8" x 13 ³/4"	(33.9cm x 35cm)
Lightweight board	1	10 ⁵/8" x 13 ³/4"	(27cm x 35cm)
Binder's boards	2	6 ¹/4" x 13 ³/8"	(22cm x 33.9cm)
Binder's boards	2	3 ³/4" x 13 ³/8"	(9.5cm x 33.9cm)
Leather	1	11 ⁵/8" x 15 ³/8"	(29.5cm x 39cm)
Book cloth	1	11" x 15 ³/8"	(27.9cm x 39cm)

Grandparent's Album

30 PAGES, 9^1/$_2$" X 6^7/$_8$" (24.1CM X 17.5CM)

The apples of their eyes

Every grandparent loves showing off photographs of their grandchildren—they'll take even more pleasure in showing off an album that their grandchildren had a hand in creating. The dimensions of this album are small enough to make it easy for elderly hands to hold.

- Be sure to include photographs of all the children and grandchildren.
- If possible, gather all the grandchildren and children together for a single photograph. Have someone outside of the family take the photograph, so that no one is left behind the camera.
- If some members of the family live far away, ask them to send recent photographs by mail or email.
- Include original drawings and special messages from the grandchildren on the interleaves.

FINAL SIZE	9 1/2" x 6 7/8"		(24.1cm x 17.5cm)
FOLD	5/8"	(1.6cm)	
PAPER WEIGHT	80 lb	(215 gsm)	

BLOCK

Papers	30	9 7/8" x 6 3/8"	(25.1cm x 16.2cm)
Interleaves	29	8 5/8" x 6 1/8"	(21.9cm x 15.6cm)
Endpapers	2	1 1/8" x 6 3/8"	(46cm x 16.2cm)
Light cotton fabric	1	5 7/8" x 2 1/2"	(6.4cm x 14.9cm)

CASE

Binder's boards	2	5 1/2" x 6 7/8"	(23cm x 17.5cm)
Lightweight board	1	5 1/2" x 6 7/8"	(19.5cm x 17.5cm)
Binder's boards	2	3 1/8" x 6 3/4"	(14cm x 17cm)
Binder's boards	2	2 3/4" x 6 3/4"	(7cm x 17cm)
Leather	1	6 1/4" x 9"	(22cm x 21cm)
Book cloth	1	4 3/4" x 9 1/2"	(19.5cm x 21cm)

Retirement Album

40 PAGES, 10¼" X 10¼" (26CM X 26CM)

Retrospective on a lifetime of achievements

When someone leaves a position they've held for twenty, thirty, or even forty years, they leave behind a lot of memories. An album full of photographs, images, texts, and other memorabilia makes an excellent parting gift. Teachers, principals, managers, and longtime employees are all excellent recipients for an album of this sort.

- Include photographs that cover all the years a person has worked with an organization. This may include photographs from special events, funny photographs, or yearbook photographs.
- Include photographs of the place of employment, such as the building exterior, the main entrance, or a person's work space.
- Print or handwrite messages from current (and former) co-workers onto the interleaves.
- Include a section devoted to wishes for the future.
- Gather together the employees who are presenting the album in a group photograph.

FINAL SIZE		**10 ^{1}/4" x 10 ^{1}/4"**	**(26cm x 26cm)**
FOLD		^{3}/4" **(2cm)**	
PAPER WEIGHT		**80 lb (215 gsm)**	

BLOCK

Papers	40	10 ^{7}/8" x 9 ^{7}/8"	(27.6cm x 25.1cm)
Interleaves	39	9 ^{1}/2" x 9 ^{1}/2"	(24.1cm x 24.1cm)
Endpapers	2	19 ^{5}/8" x 9 ^{7}/8"	(49.8cm x 25.1cm)
Light cotton fabric	1	2 ^{3}/4" x 9"	(7cm x 22.8cm)

CASE

Binder's boards	2	10" x 10 ^{1}/4"	(25.5cm x 26cm)
Lightweight board	1	9 ^{1}/4" x 10 ^{1}/4"	(23.5cm x 26cm)
Binder's boards	2	6" x 10"	(15.2cm x 25.5cm)
Binder's boards	2	3 ^{3}/8" x 10"	(8.6cm x 25.5cm)
Leather	1	10 ^{1}/4" x 11 ^{7}/8"	(26cm x 30.1cm)
Book cloth	1	7 ^{7}/8" x 11 ^{7}/8"	(20cm x 30.1cm)

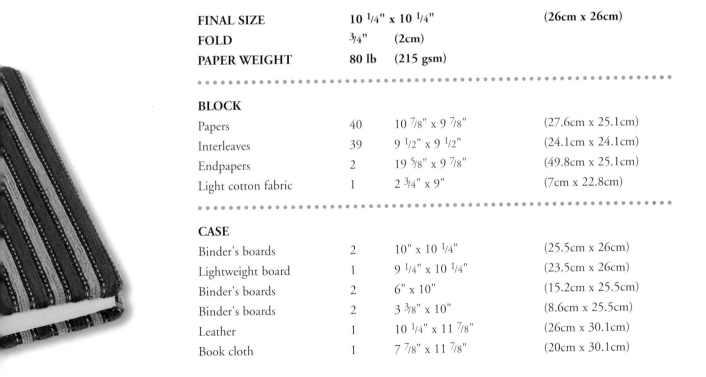

Long Trip

30 PAGES, $16^1/8$" X $11^7/8$" (41CM X 30.2CM)

Relive the adventure with every page

People often come home from long journeys with several hundred photographs. A beautiful album helps preserve the memories, and makes it easier to evoke them at will. I suggest making a panoramic album for travel photography, as landscape shots look particularly impressive when set up in this format. Compiling this album may mean throwing away a lot of photographs (or at least storing some in a shoebox) but the resulting book will be a masterpiece.

- Keep the album in mind as you travel. Save items such as ticket stubs, museum receipts, scraps of newspaper (in various languages), candy wrappers, and paper currency for photocopying onto interleaves or pasting onto pages.
- If the journey includes several countries, photocopy a map of each country or images associated with that country on the interleaf preceding that country's photographs.

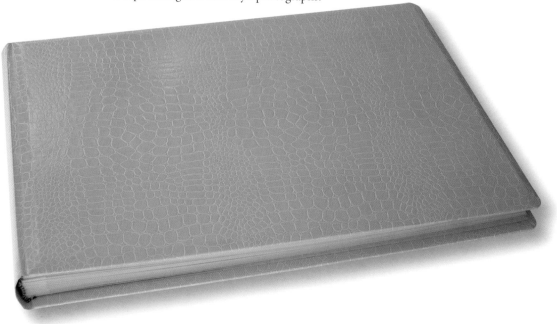

FINAL SIZE	16 1/8" x 11 7/8"		(41cm x 30.2cm)
FOLD	3/4"	(2cm)	
PAPER WEIGHT	80 lb	(215 gsm)	

BLOCK

Papers	30	16 1/2" x 11"	(41.9cm x 27.9cm)
Interleaves	29	15" x 10 5/8"	(38.1cm x 27cm)
Endpapers	2	31 1/2" x 11"	(80cm x 27.9cm)
Light cotton fabric	1	2 3/4" x 9 1/4"	(7cm x 23.5cm)

CASE

Binder's boards	2	15 3/4" x 11 3/4"	(40cm x 29.8cm)
Lightweight board	1	6 3/4" x 11 3/4"	(17.1cm x 29.8cm)
Binder's boards	2	11 3/8" x 11"	(28.9cm x 27.9cm)
Book cloth	1	35 7/8" x 13 5/8"	(91.1cm x 34cm)

Short Trip

30 PAGES, 9^1/$_2$" X 6^7/$_8$" (24.1CM X 17.5CM)

A week (and a world) away

A one- or two-week trip probably won't generate enough photographs to fill a large photograph album, but that doesn't mean it doesn't merit its own album. This panoramic version is perfect for holding photographs from a really special vacation.

- Take photographs with the album in mind during your trip. These could include shots of a hotel you stayed in—or dreamed of staying in!
- Collect ticket stubs, museum receipts, and other paper paraphernalia for interspersing in your album.
- Include portraits as well as landscape shots. You want to remember the people on your trip, as well as the sights that were seen.

FINAL SIZE	9 1/2" x 6 7/8"		(24.1cm x 17.5cm)
FOLD	5/8"	(1.6cm)	
PAPER WEIGHT	80 lb	(215 gsm)	

BLOCK

Papers	30	9 7/8" x 6 3/8"	(25.1cm x 16.2cm)
Interleaves	29	8 5/8" x 6 1/8"	(21.9cm x 15.6cm)
Endpapers	2	1 1/8" x 6 3/8"	(46cm x 16.2cm)
Light cotton fabric	1	5 7/8" x 2 1/2"	(6.4cm x 14.9cm)

CASE

Binder's boards	2	5 1/2" x 6 7/8"	(23cm x 17.5cm)
Lightweight board	1	5 1/2" x 6 7/8"	(19.5cm x 17.5cm)
Binder's boards	2	3 1/8" x 6 3/4"	(14cm x 17cm)
Binder's boards	2	2 3/4" x 6 3/4"	(7cm x 17cm)
Leather	1	6 1/4" x 9"	(22cm x 21cm)
Book cloth	1	4 3/4" x 9 1/2"	(19.5cm x 21cm)

Special Event

Large

40 PAGES, 15³/4" X 15¹/2" (40CM X 39.4CM)

Invitations to dessert—and everything in between

This album is significant and impressive. It is perfect for commemorating really special occasions, such as company milestones and large celebrations. If you are planning a very large wedding, this album may be the right size for housing photographs of the event. You will need about 500 photographs to fill this album, so make sure that is possible before embarking on this project.

- If the event relates to a company, photocopy the company logo onto the interleaves.
- If the event includes printed invitations, paste one onto one of the front pages in the album.
- Choose materials that reflect the opulence of the event. This may include really elegant fabric or particularly supple leather.
- Glue three sides of a piece of paper to the endpaper on the top of the album to make an envelope for storing a DVD of the affair.
- Create large collages of images such as food and decorations.

FINAL SIZE	15 ¾" x 15 ½"		(40cm x 39.4cm)
FOLD	¾"	(2cm)	
PAPER WEIGHT	80 lb	(215 gsm)	

BLOCK

Papers	40	15 ¾" x 15"	(40cm x 38.1cm)
Interleaves	39	14 ⅛" x 14 ⅜"	(35.9cm x 36.5cm)
Endpapers	2	30" x 15"	(76.2cm x 38.1cm)
Light cotton fabric	1	2 ¾" x 13 ¾"	(7cm x 35cm)

CASE

Binder's boards	2	15 ½" x 15 ½"	(39.4cm x 39.4cm)
Lightweight board	1	10 ⅝" x 15 ½"	(27cm x 39.4cm)
Binder's boards	2	10 ⅜" x 15 ⅛"	(26.4cm x 38.4cm)
Binder's boards	2	4" x 15 ⅛"	(10.1cm x 38.4cm)
Leather	1	11 ⅝" x 17 ½"	(29.5cm x 44.5cm)
Book cloth	1	12 ¾" x 17 ⅛"	(32.4cm x 43.5cm)

General Purpose

40 PAGES, 10¼" X 10¼" (26CM X 26CM)

A collage of recollections

Handmade photograph albums make excellent gifts for really good friends, or for yourself. A general purpose album is great for collecting photographs from holidays, weekend trips, birthday parties, and other occasions.

- Use pleasant colors that you'll be happy to look at time and again.
- Don't feel you need to lay out the whole album at once. Whenever you have a good number of photographs—and the right state of mind—arrange a chapter or two of pictures and enjoy.
- Make more than one of these albums at the same time. You will already have all the materials you need out, and this size is excellent for a variety of occasions.

FINAL SIZE	10 $\frac{1}{4}$" x 10 $\frac{1}{4}$"	(26cm x 26cm)
FOLD	$\frac{3}{4}$" (2cm)	
PAPER WEIGHT	80 LB (215 gsm)	

BLOCK

Papers	40	10 $\frac{7}{8}$" x 9 $\frac{7}{8}$"	(27.6cm x 25.1cm)
Interleaves	39	9 $\frac{1}{2}$" x 9 $\frac{1}{2}$"	(24.1cm x 24.1cm)
Endpapers	2	19 $\frac{5}{8}$" x 9 $\frac{7}{8}$"	(49.8cm x 25.1cm)
Light cotton fabric	1	2 $\frac{3}{4}$" x 9"	(7cm x 22.8cm)

CASE

Binder's boards	2	10" x 10 $\frac{1}{4}$"	(25.5cm x 26cm)
Lightweight board	1	9 $\frac{1}{4}$" x 10 $\frac{1}{4}$"	(23.5cm x 26cm)
Binder's boards	2	6" x 10"	(15.2cm x 25.5cm)
Binder's boards	2	3 $\frac{3}{8}$" x 10"	(8.6cm x 25.5cm)
Leather	1	10 $\frac{1}{4}$" x 11 $\frac{7}{8}$"	(26cm x 30.1cm)
Book cloth	1	7 $\frac{7}{8}$" x 11 $\frac{7}{8}$"	(20cm x 30.1cm)

Guestbook

50 PAGES, 8⅝" X 8⅝" (22.5CM X 22.5CM)

Best greetings and warmest wishes

Having a guestbook at a baby shower, wedding shower, or any other important event is a wonderful way of collecting guests' good wishes, and preserving memories of the event. This book includes 50 pages, so there is lots of room for messages of any length.

- Choose fabric that compliments the affair. For a baby shower, you'll want something colorful and fun. For a wedding shower, you'll want something that matches the colors of the wedding.
- Buy several fine-tipped markers for people to sign the album. Choose colors that coordinate with the fabric and paper.
- Use relatively light paper for the block, as it doesn't need to support any photographs. I suggest 32lb (120gsm) as an excellent weight.

FINAL SIZE	8 $\frac{5}{8}$" x 8 $\frac{5}{8}$"	(22.5cm x 22.5cm)
FOLD	$\frac{5}{8}$" (1.6cm)	
PAPER WEIGHT	32 lb (120 gsm)	

BLOCK

Papers	50	5 $\frac{1}{2}$" x 8 $\frac{1}{2}$"	(23cm x 21.6cm)
Interleaves	none		
Endpapers	2	17" x 8 $\frac{1}{2}$"	(43.2cm x 21.6cm)
Light cotton fabric	1	2" x 8 $\frac{1}{2}$"	(5cm x 21.6cm)

CASE

Binder's boards	2	8 $\frac{1}{4}$" x 8 $\frac{7}{8}$"	(21cm x 22.5cm)
Lightweight board	1	5 $\frac{1}{2}$" x 8 $\frac{7}{8}$"	(14cm x 22.5cm)
Binder's boards	2	8 $\frac{1}{4}$" x 8 $\frac{5}{8}$"	(21cm x 21.9cm)
Book cloth	1	19 $\frac{1}{2}$" x 10 $\frac{3}{8}$"	(49.5cm x 26.4cm)

Personal Diary

25 PAGES, 5³/4" X 8" (14.6CM X 20.3CM)

As personal as possible, from the very first page
This book is small and compact. It fits into knapsacks, handbags, and briefcases, making it a perfect accompaniment for trips. It is also a handy size for keeping on a bedside table to record dreams and other nighttime thoughts.

- Paste items such as subway maps, ticket stubs, or museum receipts in the pages of this book.
- Include business cards from really good restaurants that you'll want to visit again.
- Use off-white paper for the block so that this diary can double as a sketchbook. You don't need to be an artist to draw pictorial reminders of interesting sights.

FINAL SIZE	5 3/4" x 8"		(14.6cm x 20.3cm)
FOLD	1/2"	(1.3cm)	
PAPER WEIGHT	80 lb	(215 gsm)	

Block

Papers	25	5 7/8" x 7 1/2"	(14.9cm x 19cm)
Interleaves	none		
Endpapers	2	10 5/8" x 7 1/2"	(27cm x 19cm)
Light cotton fabric	1	5 3/4" x 7"	(14.6cm x 18cm)

CASE

Binder's boards	2	5 1/2" x 7 7/8"	(14cm x 20cm)
Lightweight board	1	5 1/2" x 7 7/8"	(14cm x 20cm)
Binder's boards	2	3 1/8" x 7 3/4"	(8cm x 19.7cm)
Binder's boards	2	1 5/8" x 7 3/4"	(4.1cm x 19.7cm)
Leather	1	6 1/4" x 9"	(15.9cm x 22.9cm)
Book cloth	1	4 3/4" x 9 1/2"	(12cm x 24.1cm)

Graduation Album

30 PAGES, 10¹⁄₄" X 10¹⁄₄" (26CM X 26CM)

An achievement worthy of remembering

Whether they are at the end of high school or the culmination of a university degree, graduations are important. They signify achievement after a period of hard work, dedication, and personal growth. A handmade album commemorating this special occasion—and the years that led to its fulfillment—makes a perfect graduation gift. For someone moving to a faraway college or new job, this album is an excellent parting gift.

- Include photographs taken throughout the period of study. If it commemorates a high school graduation, be sure to include pictures taken by the school photographer over the years. If it marks the end of a university or college degree, include photographs of major events that occurred during the period of study.
- Incorporate diplomas and special awards in the album. If there are personal letters from teachers, coaches, and friends, you can include these as well.
- Photocopy the school logo onto an interleaf.

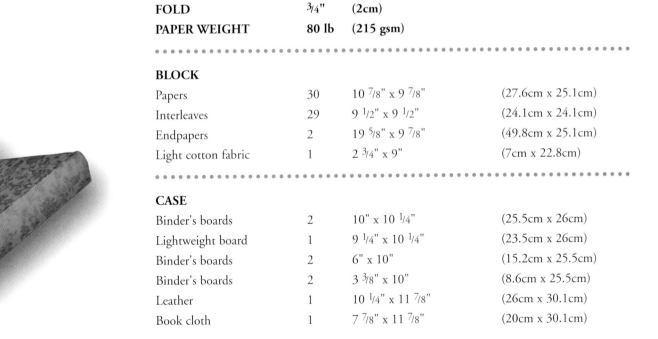

FINAL SIZE	10 $^1/_4$" x 10 $^1/_4$"	(26cm x 26cm)
FOLD	$^3/_4$" (2cm)	
PAPER WEIGHT	80 lb (215 gsm)	

BLOCK

Papers	30	10 $^7/_8$" x 9 $^7/_8$"	(27.6cm x 25.1cm)
Interleaves	29	9 $^1/_2$" x 9 $^1/_2$"	(24.1cm x 24.1cm)
Endpapers	2	19 $^5/_8$" x 9 $^7/_8$"	(49.8cm x 25.1cm)
Light cotton fabric	1	2 $^3/_4$" x 9"	(7cm x 22.8cm)

CASE

Binder's boards	2	10" x 10 $^1/_4$"	(25.5cm x 26cm)
Lightweight board	1	9 $^1/_4$" x 10 $^1/_4$"	(23.5cm x 26cm)
Binder's boards	2	6" x 10"	(15.2cm x 25.5cm)
Binder's boards	2	3 $^3/_8$" x 10"	(8.6cm x 25.5cm)
Leather	1	10 $^1/_4$" x 11 $^7/_8$"	(26cm x 30.1cm)
Book cloth	1	7 $^7/_8$" x 11 $^7/_8$"	(20cm x 30.1cm)

Collector's Album

50 PAGES, 8⅝" X 8⅝" (22.5CM X 22.5CM)

A personal portfolio of art and ideas

This album is a catchall for people who love to collect. Small enough to fit into a briefcase or large handbag, it can be carried around daily and used to hold thoughts and observations, remarkable images and experiences. Unlike a fancy storage box, this collection of treasures is easy to browse through, and can be stored inconspicuously on a bookshelf.

- Integrate a variety of paper types in this album. You may want to divide the album into sections, so that one type of paper is used for holding photographs, another type is used for sketching, and a third type is used for handwritten messages.
- Incorporate diverse materials including special photographs, pieces of fabric, unusual magazine ads, and anything else that strikes your fancy.
- This book is also a collection of thoughts as well as objects. Include personal reflections and notable quotes as well.

Collections, N.Y.

FINAL SIZE		8 ⁵⁄₈" x 8 ⁵⁄₈"	**(22.5cm x 22.5cm)**
FOLD		⁵⁄₈" **(1.6cm)**	
PAPER WEIGHT		**32 lb (120 gsm)**	

BLOCK

Papers	50	5 ¹⁄₂" x 8 ¹⁄₂"	(23cm x 21.6cm)
Interleaves	none		
Endpapers	2	17" x 8 ¹⁄₂"	(43.2cm x 21.6cm)
Light cotton fabric	1	2" x 8 ¹⁄₂"	(5cm x 21.6cm)

CASE

Binder's boards	2	8 ¹⁄₄" x 8 ⁷⁄₈"	(21cm x 22.5cm)
Lightweight board	1	5 ¹⁄₂" x 8 ⁷⁄₈"	(14cm x 22.5cm)
Binder's boards	2	8 ¹⁄₄" x 8 ⁵⁄₈"	(21cm x 21.9cm)
Book cloth	1	19 ¹⁄₂" x 10 ³⁄₈"	(49.5cm x 26.4cm)

Tips of the Trade

Start Simple

Making an album is a demanding process, one that requires precision and patience. I recommend concentrating on the fundamentals for your first few albums. As you become familiar with the materials and techniques, integrate upgrades such as decorated interleaves and other personalized touches.

Stock up!

Making a photograph album takes forethought and planning. Since many of the materials have to be purchased from specialty shops, I suggest buying enough material for several albums at once. This also means you'll have spare parts on hand if you make a mistake.

Plan for the Future

Each stage of the process requires a different array of materials and tools. Each stage is also connected with a different pace and disposition. I recommend making some items in bulk. For example, I usually prepare several book cloths at once. Not only do I have all the supplies I need on hand, but I am also in the mood.

Stick with One Size

Don't overwhelm yourself with dimensions. If you decide to make more than one album at a time, make all of them the same size. Having too many sizes of board, paper, fabric, and leather can get downright confusing!

Moderation

The number of pages you put in your album is an important consideration. Albums that have too many pages may be difficult to fill—since you want your album to be a complete story, you don't want empty pages at the end. From a practical perspective, albums with lots of pages may be

difficult to hold. If there's one thing you want people to do with these albums, it's hold them! Albums that have too few pages can be disappointing. Considering all the work that goes into preparing an album, it's a shame if it only accommodates a few pictures.

Tools

*M*ost of these tools can be found at major art supplies stores or bookbinding shops. The internet is an excellent source for finding exactly what you need—most suppliers can deliver straight to your door.

Acrylic board Use this as an intermediary medium for applying glue to make the book cloth. You can also use a piece of glass, mirror, or any other large, flat surface that is smooth and easy to clean.

Acrylic drawer Use this to line up paper while creasing and gluing the block. Any open box with three vertical sides and 90° corners that can hold papers in a straight stack is fine, but an acrylic drawer is particularly handy since it is easy to clean. A single size can be used for albums of several different sizes, just tape a piece of cardboard to make a temporary border.

Bone folder This is the pride of every bookbinder—his or her right (or left) hand. Bone folders today may be made from a variety of materials; whatever type you select, make sure it has flat sides and is comfortable to hold. Your bone holder shouldn't be too sharp, as that can damage the paper; it shouldn't be too dull, as it must reinforce folds. Keep your bone folder clean and free from glue or dirt.

Brushes Use clean, high quality brushes that don't shed hairs. A round brush is best for spreading glue on large surfaces. Use a flat brush for applying glue to the spine. A small brush can be used to spread glue on paper for making photograph frames. Remember to clean brushes **immediately** after use so that the glue doesn't dry.

Most of these tools can be found at major art supplies stores or bookbinding shops. The internet is an excellent source for finding exactly what you need—most suppliers can deliver straight to your door.

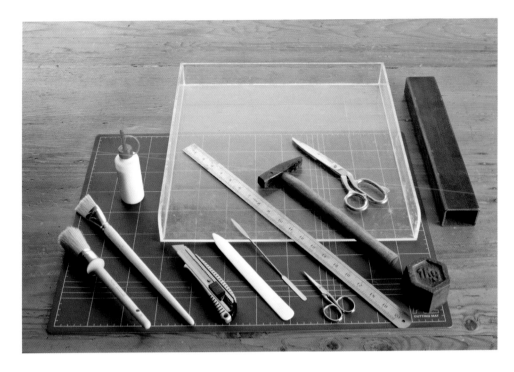

Tools for building the block and case. From left to right: Round brush, Flat brush, Small plastic bottle, Craft knife, Bone folder, Microspatula, Small scissors, Metal ruler, Small hammer, Small weight, Fabric scissors, Large weight, Cutting mat, Acrylic drawer.

Craft knives The knife you use to cut leather should be sharp and precise. The knife you use to cut board should be sturdy and heavy. Knives with removable blades are best, as dull blades can be replaced.

Cutting mat You'll want to have a large one of these for cutting leather and board. Use a self-healing mat that has rulers along at least two edges.

Double-sided glue dots These handy adhesive circles are used to secure photographs onto the pages of your album. Make sure you select glue dots that are acid-free. You'll also want to choose relatively small dots, so they don't cause your photographs to bulge on the page.

Glue Select strong glue that dries quickly and is non-acidic. The most commonly used glue is PVA (Polyvinyl Acetate), a general purpose adhesive that is transparent when dry. PVA can be used to glue paper, board, cloth, and leather. Jade 403 and YES are two popular brands of glue used in bookbinding.

Paper cutter This sharp device is used to cut paper neatly and quickly. Use it to trim photographs precisely, or for cutting paper frames for your photographs.

Headpins These small pins are used to secure thin headbands in place while applying glue.

Metal ruler This is used for cutting straight edges in leather and paper. Use a metal ruler rather than a plastic one so you don't have to worry about cutting the ruler with your knife.

Microspatula This small tool acts as an extension of your fingers, enabling you to work glue into small spaces. If you can't get your hands on a miscrospatula, try using half of a pair of scissors.

Scissors Keep a variety of scissors on hand, as each type has its own special purpose. Use *heavy fabric scissors* for cutting fabric and book cloth. Use *small scissors* for trimming photographs. You may want to have a pair of *paper shaper* scissors as well. These have patterned blades that cut attractive edges for photograph frames.

Small hammer Any lightweight hammer can be used to tap book cloth and leather onto the case. Tapping helps smooth the materials once they are glued to the binder's boards.

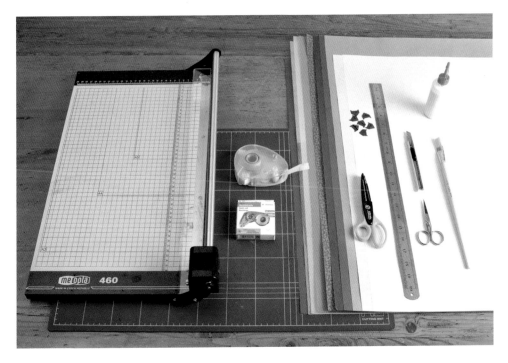

Tools for arranging the photographs. From left to right: Paper cutter, Cutting mat, Small craft knife, Paper shaper scissors, Small scissors, Double-sided glue dots and dispenser, Metal ruler, Small brush, Mounting corners, Small plastic bottle, Mounting papers.

Small plastic bottle Though this item may be small, its importance is great, as it allows you to apply glue in tiny, precise lines. Small bottles used for hair coloring are perfect—look for them at cosmetic supply stores. Make sure your bottle has a tight-fitting cap so that the glue doesn't dry up between uses.

Weights You'll need at least one or two weights to hold down papers and fabric while waiting for glue to dry. Long weights are excellent for holding down glued edges. If you are using small weights, lay boards under the weight to diffuse its effect. If the weight you are using has sharp edges, wrap the weight in fabric so that it doesn't dent the paper.

Materials

All of the materials in a handmade photograph album are chosen in accord with each other, just as all the instruments in an ensemble are tuned to play in harmony. One choice influences another, and is connected to it. The leather and fabric used for the case should compliment each other. Both of these materials must be in tune with the paper in the block, and the interleaves. The color, texture, and nature of all the materials must be complimentary and melodious.

Paper

A variety of papers are used in the construction of your photograph album. Here are a few general comments about the nature of this essential substance.

Grain Paper is made up of fibers. Grain is the direction in which most of the fibers in a single piece of paper are aligned. The simplest way of testing grain direction is by folding the paper in half. Paper offers more resistance when it is folded against the grain. **When orienting paper for your album, you want the grain to run parallel to the spine.** When grain is parallel to the longer side of the paper, it is called **long grain**. If you are making a panoramic album; that is, if the width of the album is greater than its height, you'll need to use **short grain** paper. This means the grain is parallel to the short side of the paper.

Acidity One of the most important things to consider when selecting paper for a photograph album is its acidity. Paper that contains acid will harm photographs over time, as the acid reacts with the chemicals in the photographs. Acidity in paper is often marked on the package. Test paper acidity yourself with a pH pen, available in most art supply stores.

Weight Two systems are used for describing a paper's weight. In the United States, the system is based on the weight in pounds per 500 sheets of paper in a specific size. The international system for weighing paper is more standardized.

It is based on the weight in grams per square meter of paper. According to this system, all paper, regardless of size, is weighed in the same manner.

Paper for the block

This is the paper that supports and displays your photographs, the paper you'll be using to build the block. When choosing this paper, there are three major issues to consider: weight, color, and texture.

Weight Each page in the album must be strong enough to support several photographs. Paper that is too heavy will make the album unwieldy; paper that is too light will bend under the weight of the photographs. I suggest using paper with a weight of 80lb (215gsm) for photograph albums. If you are making a personal diary or guestbook (pages 42 and 40) use lighter paper, something with a weight of 32lb (120gsm). **Paper weight affects the width of the spine—the heavier the paper, the thicker the spine.**

Color In the past, there were two options for paper color in photograph albums: white or black. People tended to contrast the color of the book cloth with the color of the block. Light book cloth was combined with black paper, and vice versa. Thank heavens things have changed! Nowadays, any color (or combination of colors) can be used in photograph albums. The decision about paper color should be made in conjunction with choices regarding book cloth and leather. You may wish to use different shades of the same color for all three elements, or draw out colors in the fabric through your choice of paper color.

Texture Paper comes in both smooth and rough varieties. I suggest opting for rough paper in the block, as it has much more personality and beauty than smooth paper. Rough paper is also pleasant to the touch, adding a sensual dimension to your album.

Kraft paper

This simple brown paper is pasted onto the wrong side of fabric to make book cloth. Its purpose is to connect the fabric to the case—it adds stability to the fabric, but shouldn't detract from the fabric's flexibility or softness.

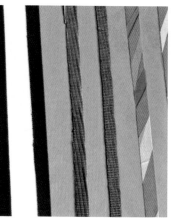

Cardboard

Stiffer and more durable than regular paper, cardboard is used to construct the case of your photograph album. Scrap pieces of cardboard are used to distribute weight when gluing materials, and for securing papers in place while you work.

Binder's board is heavy cardboard used to construct the front and back of the case. Choose a brand that is acid-free and warp-resistant. Binder's board is often sold in standard sizes. These may not match the photograph album you envision; in such cases, cut the board yourself using a heavy craft knife and metal ruler. Binder's board is usually cut with straight corners. Rounded corners on the outer edges of the board give the album a softer look.

Lightweight board is used to cover the spine. Choose a board that is more flexible than binder's board, as it must curve gently around the spine of the block.

Interleaf

Photographs that are in contact with other photographs become damaged over time; to avoid this, interleaves are placed between the pages in your photograph album. A variety of materials can be used as interleaf. Glassine is a thin, lightweight, glossy material made of 100% sulphate. It is acid-free, impenetrable to oil and grease, and highly resistant to solvents and chemicals. Standard glassine is white, but it comes in a variety of colors, and with various textures and designs. Tissue paper and tracing paper can also be used as interleaf.

These materials have an advantage over glassine, as they can be run through printers and photo-copying machines, or decorated with permanent markers. Whatever material you use to separate the photographs in you album, make sure it is acid-free, flexible, soft, and does not crease easily.

Leather

The material you use to cover the spine of your photograph album is particularly important, as this is the first element that will be visible when your album rests on a bookshelf. Be sure to choose leather that is beautiful to the eyes, and pleasant to the touch. Leather comes from a variety of animals, and the width of various leathers differs. You'll want leather that is relatively thin, so that it folds easily over the case and wraps smoothly around the spine. I recommend choosing something that is no wider than $1/16$" (0.15cm). Delicate lamb leather, for example, is better than thick cow leather. Be sure to select a piece of leather that is smooth and free from marks or faults.

Fabric

Book cloth Colorful and bright. Staid and serious. Elegant, rich, playful, or sentimental. The fabric you transform into book cloth makes a huge impression on the style of your album. Even before someone begins to flip through its pages, they will encounter this tangible, colorful, sensual element. Book cloth is fabric that has paper glued to one side. Book

cloth is sold readymade at many bookbinding supply shops, but it is easy to make using regular fabric, Kraft paper, and glue. Making it yourself frees your imagination, allowing you to use almost any fabric you want.

The main parameters dictating the type of fabric used to make book cloth are thickness and flexibility. The fabric must be glued to paper, so using really thin fabrics such as silk or lace is impractical, as it will be permeated by the glue. On the other hand, you don't want fabric that is too thick, as book cloth must fold nicely at the corners, and thick fabric may be inflexible.

Aside from these parameters, any fabric can be used as book cloth. Upholstery fabric, old curtains, a favorite skirt, or a tablecloth you don't use anymore are all excellent sources for making book cloth. Before transforming fabric into book cloth, be sure the fabric is clean and ironed.

Spine liner You'll need a piece of thin cotton fabric such as muslin for lining the spine. This fabric need not be fancy as it is concealed by the case. Its function is to reinforce the adhesion between of the papers in the block and the endpaper. It also acts as a connector between the block and the case.

Headband

These colorful striped bands, also known as endbands, are glued at the top and bottom of the spine. An important component in early bookbinding, these bands were originally composed of the threads used to sew books. Today, their purpose is primarily aesthetic, as they hide imperfections in the spine, and evoke traditional bookbinding techniques.

Techniques for Building the Album

You've decided upon the purpose of your album, settled upon the dimensions, and gathered your materials. Now you're ready to begin building. Put on some excellent music (I recommend a powerful symphonic concert), roll up your sleeves, and prepare to embark on a project that will bring you joy, pride, and satisfaction for many years to come.

The album described in the following pages measures 10 1/4" x 10 1/4" (26cm x 26cm). For alternate dimensions, select one of the album types described on pages 10 to 46.

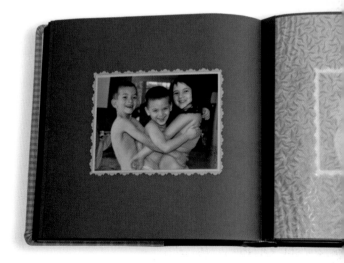

Preparing the book cloth

Make the book cloth first, so that it has time to dry while other elements of the album are being prepared. The process involves gluing Kraft paper to the wrong side of fabric. It can be a little messy, but if you work carefully and methodically, you'll be able to apply the glue evenly and neatly.

Materials

- Two 8 ¹/₂" x 12 ¹/₂" (21.6cm x 31.8cm) sheets of Kraft paper
- Two 8" x 12" (20.3cm x 30.5cm) pieces of fabric
- Acrylic board, larger than your fabric
- Two pieces of cardboard, larger than your fabric
- Weight
- Glue
- Round brush

Instructions

1. Place the acrylic board on your work surface. Place the fabric wrong-side up on a piece of cardboard.

2. Spread a thick layer of glue evenly on the acrylic board, covering an area that is larger than the area of the paper.

3. Place a sheet of paper on the glue, laying it flat and pressing it with your fingertips to ensure the glue reaches every corner of the paper.

4. When you are confident that the glue has reached all the corners, grasp adjacent corners of the paper and lift. Do this quickly, as you don't want the glue to dry while the paper is on the board.

5. Line up the corners of the paper with the corners of the fabric and place the paper glue-side down on the fabric. Rub the paper with your hand so that it lies flat on the fabric.

Tip

When cutting fabric for the book cloth, make sure it is slightly larger than the book cloth you'll need. The Kraft paper should be slightly larger than the fabric. After the fabric has been glued to the paper, trim the book cloth to the exact size you need for your album.

6. Lay a piece of cardboard on top of the paper, and place a weight over top. You should now have a pile of fabric, glue, and paper sandwiched between two pieces of cardboard. The boards absorb moisture from the glue, ensuring that the fabric and paper lie flat as the glue dries.

7. Repeat Steps 1 to 6 to transform the other fabric into book cloth.

Tip
I recommend preparing several pieces of book cloth at one time. Once you have the materials on hand and have found your work rhythm, you'll find the process simply flows.

8. Set aside to dry overnight.
9. When the book cloth is dry, trim each piece to a size of 7 7/8" x 11 1/2" (20cm x 30.1cm).

Creasing and folding the paper

The first stage in preparing the block involves creasing and folding the papers. This must be done carefully and precisely, as you want each paper to remain identical even after folding. The technique described below is simple—it requires nothing more complicated that a piece of cardboard, masking tape, a straight edge, and a bone tool.

Materials

- Forty 10 ⅞" x 9 ⅞" (27.6cm x 25.1cm) sheets of paper
- One piece of cardboard
- Masking tape
- Acrylic drawer
- Metal ruler
- Weight

Instructions

1. Place the acrylic drawer on your work surface. Measure the height of your final paper size from the open edge of the drawer. In this case, you'll measure 9 ³/₄" (24.8cm) from the edge. Make a pocket by taping a piece of cardboard at this point in the drawer. This pocket provides a border for lining up each paper for creasing.

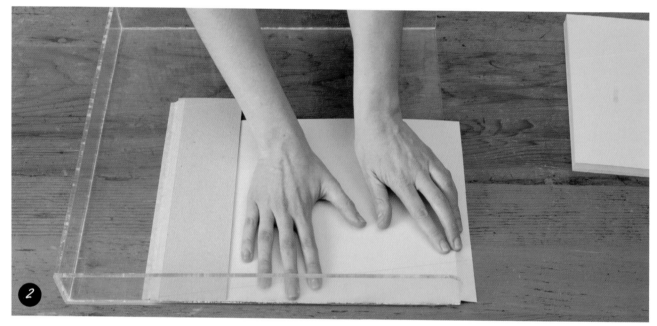

2. Slide a paper into the drawer, pressing it into the pocket. Crease the edge of the paper that hangs over the edge of the drawer.

3. Remove the paper and set aside.

4. Repeat Steps 2 and 3 to crease all 40 papers.

5. Reinforce the crease in each paper by pressing down on the fold with your fingers.

Tip
This process is soothing and meditative. It requires peace of mind and rhythm. For me, it connects with classical music—a favorite piano or violin concerto.

6. Reinforce each fold by running the bone folder along the edge of the fold.

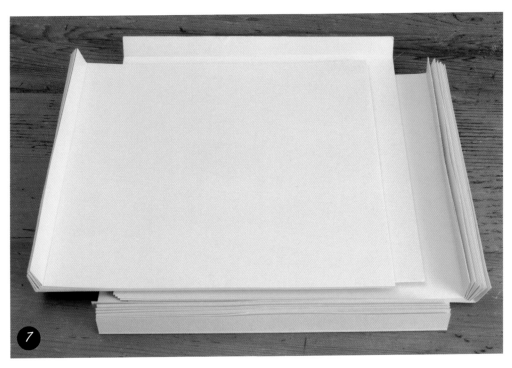

7. Stack the folded papers in piles of ten.

Gluing the block

This is an intensive process that requires concentration and patience. The process is also time-consuming, so if you need to take a break, do so. It's a shame to make an imperfect block just because you ran out of time or lost focus. Place a weight on the glued edge of the papers if you do take a break, as that will keep the pages condensed as they dry.

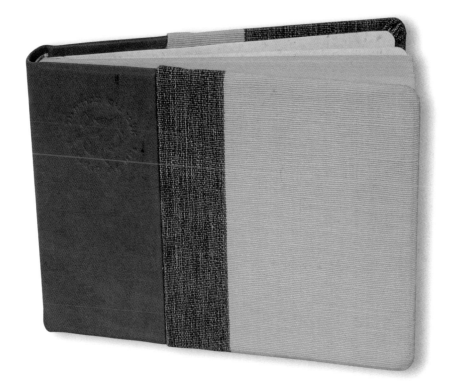

Materials

- Forty sheets of paper, each folded to 9 $\frac{3}{4}$" x 9 $\frac{7}{8}$" (24.8cm x 25.1cm)
- Thirty-nine 9 $\frac{1}{2}$" x 9 $\frac{1}{2}$" (24.1cm x 24.1cm) sheets of interleaf
- Glue
- Acrylic drawer
- Small plastic bottle
- Flat brush
- Weight

Instructions

1. Place the drawer on your work surface and orient it so that the open end faces you. Lay a paper in the drawer, with the folded side facing upwards and closest to you. Press the paper snugly into the left corner of the drawer. Lay a straight weight along the right side of the paper to secure it in place.

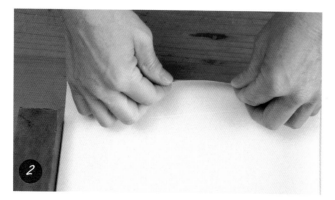

2. Refold the folded edge, first with your fingers.

3. Then with the bone folder.

Tip

There is a great feeling in the culmination of this process, as one has transformed pieces of paper and interleaves into a unified whole with substance and weight.

4. Apply a thin line of glue along the folded edge of the paper. Take care that the glue is closer to the edge of the paper rather than the fold.

5. Also, ensure that there is no glue at the corners of the paper. The interleaves are smaller than the paper and won't reach the corners.

6. Grasp adjacent corners of an interleaf with both hands. Carefully lay it on the paper, taking care that the edge of the interleaf is straight and even with the folded edge of the paper. Do not pull or stretch the interleaf after it has been laid on the glue. Once the interleaf is wet, it can rip or tear easily.

7. Press your fingers gently and evenly along the seam of glue connecting the interleaf and the paper.

10. Lay a sheet of paper onto the glue, lining up its folded edge with the folded edge of the previous paper.

11. Repeat Steps 2 to 8 to glue ten papers and ten interleaves together. Remove the set from the drawer, place a weight along the glued edge, and set aside.

12. Repeat Steps 1 to 9 to make three more sets of papers and interleaves. The last set will have just nine interleaves, and will end with a paper.

13. Glue all four sets together, placing the nine-interleaf set at the top, to form a block with forty pages and thirty-nine interleaves.

14. Place a weight on the glued edge of the block and set aside to dry.

8. Apply a fine line of glue along the edge of the interleaf.

> *Tip*
>
> *Building the block is a concert of movements whose melody is soothing and meditative. It goes something like this: Lay paper. Reinforce fold. Apply glue. Place interleaf. Apply glue. Lay paper. Reinforce fold. Apply glue. Place interleaf. Apply glue. Lay paper.*

9. Apply a parallel line of glue along the edge of the paper. These two lines of glue will hold the next sheet of paper. Again, take care not to apply glue to the corners of the paper, as you don't want the glue to ooze over the edges, damaging the other papers and interleaf.

Adding endpapers

To transform a block into the interior of an album, folded pieces of paper are attached to the front and back of the block. These are called endpapers. They are twice as wide as each folded page in the block, and identical in height.

Materials

- Glued block
- Two 19 $\frac{5}{8}$" x 9 $\frac{7}{8}$" (49.8cm x 25.1cm) sheets of paper
- Glue
- Small plastic bottle

Instructions

1. Place the block right-side up on your work surface. Fold each sheet of paper in half widthwise.

2. Apply a thin line of glue along the folded edge of the block.

3. Line up the folded edge of the endpaper with the folded edge of the block. Press down firmly along the edge to secure.

4. Turn over the block so the bottom faces up, and apply glue along the folded edge. Line up the folded edge of the other endpaper with the folded edge on this side of the block and press down firmly to secure.

5. Place a weight on the glued edge of the block and set aside to dry.

Tip

I usually use the same type of paper for the endpapers as I use for the block. You may choose other paper as well—just be sure the two types of paper suit each other in color and texture.

Lining the spine

The spine of the album, like the spine of the body, holds everything in place. It must be stable, strong, and straight. A well-built spine allows pages to spread flat, almost panoramically, when the album is open. Though the spine has to be strong, it must also be flexible. The fabric used to line it must be soft, and the glue must be applied with a light hand.

Materials

- Block with endpapers
- One 2 ³/₄" x 9" (7cm x 22.8cm) piece of light cotton fabric
- Glue
- Small plastic bottle
- Flat brush
- Bone folder

Instructions

1. Apply thin lines of glue along the spine of the block.

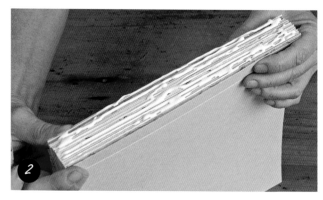

2. Do not apply glue at the top or bottom edges, as the fabric you are gluing is slightly shorter than the block.

3. Spread the glue evenly along the spine.

4. Ensure that there is glue on every piece of paper, as this glue helps keep the papers together.

Tip

The height of the fabric used to line the spine should be slightly shorter than the album. As for the width, it should be about ³/₄" (2cm) wider than the spine, so that it can wrap overlap a little on the front and back endpapers.

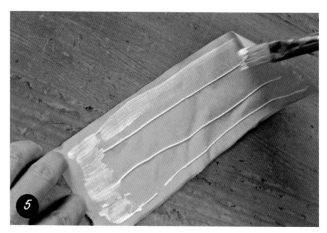

5. Apply lines of glue to the fabric and spread evenly all over the fabric. Don't worry if the glue on the spine dries a little as you apply glue to the fabric.

6. Lay the block along a long edge of the fabric, so that a flap of fabric measuring $3/8$" (1 cm) lies under the block. Grasp the fabric with both hands and draw it upwards and over the spine. Press the fabric against the spine as you wrap.

7. Apply a thin line of glue along the edge of the front of the block.

8. Wrap the fabric over, pressing the flap evenly along the line of glue.

9. Carefully turn over the block and apply a thin line of glue along the edge. Press down the flap of fabric.

10. While the glue is still wet, use a bone folder to press the fabric against the spine. Tuck the fabric into the grooves to ensure that every paper in the block is glued to the fabric.

11. Place a weight along the glued edge of the block and set aside to dry.

Tip

An album with a spine constructed in this manner is durable and strong. It can withstand lots of curious hands flipping through back and forth, and be passed down from generation to generation with pride.

Adding headbands

These striped bands conceal imperfections in your block and evoke classic traditions relating to bookmaking.

Materials

- One 4" (10cm) piece of headband
- Block with lined spine
- Piece of cardboard
- Headpins
- Glue
- Flat brush

Instructions

1. Place the headband on a piece of cardboard. Secure each end of the headband with a headpin.

2. Apply glue along half of the headband. You'll be cutting the headband in two pieces, with one piece wrapping around the top of the spine and the other half around the bottom, so apply the glue in sections.

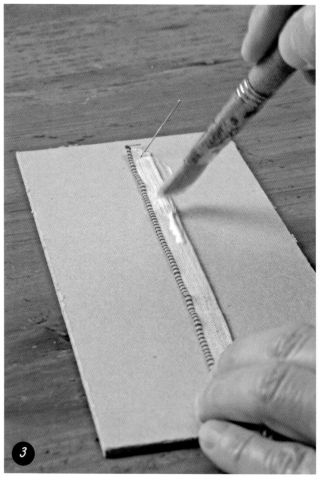

3. Spread the glue with a flat brush.

Tip

With 40 folded pages and 39 interleaves, you're destined to have a few irregularities in your block. These colorful bands make excellent camouflage.

4. Cut the headband and wrap it around the top of the spine, making sure it overlaps slightly on both endpapers. Orient the headband so that the colored edge faces upwards. It should be horizontal over the spine and angle slightly downwards on the front and back endpapers.

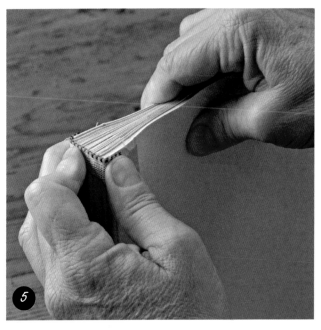

Tip

With the application of the headband, the block is prepared. A unified whole has been assembled from pieces of paper and interleaves. The first block is the hardest, as you are discovering the art of creasing, folding, and gluing. As you gain experience, you'll find other blocks much easier to prepare, though the results will be no less rewarding.

5. Press the headband firmly with your fingers to secure.
6. Apply glue to the other half of the headband and paste at the other end of the block, so that the colored edge faces downwards.
7. Place a weight on the glued edge of the block and set aside to dry for at least 24 hours.

Building the case

The album case is composed of seven boards. Double layers of binder's boards make up the front and back covers—this increases the durability of your album, helping to ensure it doesn't buckle over time. A single piece of lightweight board connects the front and back covers, and bends gently to cover the spine of the block.

Materials

- Two 10" x 10 1/4" (25.5cm x 26cm) pieces of binder's board
- Two 6" x 10" (15.2cm x 25.5cm) pieces of binder's board
- Two 3 3/8" x 10" (8.6cm x 25.5cm) pieces of binder's board
- One 9 1/4" x 10 1/4" (23.5cm x 26cm) piece of lightweight board
- Glue
- Round brush
- Metal ruler

Instructions

1. Lay the largest pieces of binder's boards on your work surface, so that the long edges face each other.

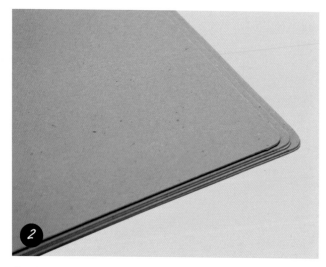

2. If your boards have rounded corners, make sure these corners face outwards. The boards should be 1¹/2" (4cm) apart; this space must be large enough to accommodate the spine of the block. Double check by measuring your block to make sure this space is large enough.

3. Spread glue wide strips along facing edges of the boards.

4. Lay the lightweight board on these boards, so that it overlaps evenly on each board. All three boards should make a continuous edge along the top and bottom—lay the boards against a straight edge or ruler to be sure.

Tip

Preparing the case is like listening to Brazilian music. Fundamental and basic. Though I am familiar with all of the elements, the finale is always a surprise. It is like a samba that remains exciting, even though I've heard it hundreds of times.

5. Spread a thin layer of glue on one of the medium binder's boards.

6. Start at the edges and working your way inwards, covering all of the board and making sure there are no clumps.

7. Place the board on the left side of the case, leaving a margin of $^{1}/16$" (0.6cm) along the top, bottom, and outer edges.

8. If you have rounded corners, make sure these corners face outwards.

9. Spread glue on the other medium board.

10. And place on the right side of the case, leaving a margin of $^1/16$" (0.6cm) along the top, bottom, and outer edges.

11. Repeat step 9.

Tip

You now have a case, albeit a bare one, for your album. Now it is time to dress the case in the book cloth and leather that have been selected for this occasion.

12. Move now to the small binder's boards, applying glue evenly to one of the boards and placing it to the left of the spine, 3/4" (1.9cm) from the board you glued in Step 7. The right edge of this board should be in line with the outer edge of the flexible lightweight board. The top and bottom edges should be even with the other boards.

14. And place on the other side of the spine, 3/4" (1.9cm) from the medium board you glued in Step 9.

13. Apply glue evenly to the other small board.

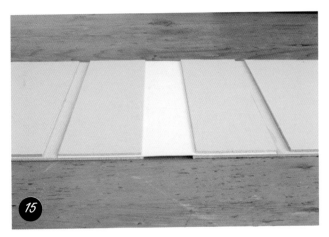

15. Ensure that all three layers are lined up evenly along the top and bottom edges.

Gluing the leather

The case of the features two large pieces of binder's board. The exterior features four binder's boards—two small boards and two medium boards. All of these boards are held together by a single piece of flexible lightweight board.

Materials

- Case
- One 10 $\frac{1}{4}$" x 11 $\frac{7}{8}$" (26cm x 30.1cm) piece of leather
- Glue
- Round brush
- Bone folder

Instructions

1. Place the case exterior-side up on your work surface. Place the leather wrong-side up on your work surface.

2. Apply glue evenly on the wrong side of the leather. Don't apply glue to the top and bottom edges.

3. Apply glue to the small binder's boards and the lightweight board connecting them.

4. Spread glue in the grooves located to the left and right of the small boards as well.

5. Grasp the leather in both hands and begin laying it on the case, starting at the side closest to you. The bottom edge of the leather doesn't have any glue yet—it should rest on your work surface as you unroll the rest of the leather onto the case. Take care that the leather is smooth and flat as you press it onto the case.

6. Use the bone folder to smooth the leather onto the boards.

7. Tuck the leather into the grooves on either side of the small boards.

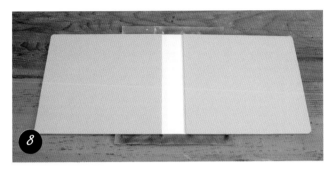

8. Turn over the case, so that the interior faces upwards. Smooth out the leather flaps at the top and bottom of the case.

9. Apply glue to the leather flap closest to you, and to the area on the case that will be covered by the flap.

10. Fold over the leather, smoothing it first with your fingers and then with the bone folder.

11. Rotate the case and repeat Steps 8 and 9 on the other side, applying glue to the leather flap and to the area on the case that will be covered by the flap.

Tip

You may want to do a dress rehearsal at this stage by placing the leather and book cloth on the case, and making sure everything fits just right before applying the glue.

12. Fold over the leather and press it carefully, first with your fingers and then with the bone folder, until smooth.

Adding the book cloth

The leather is laid, and your case is beginning to resemble the photograph album you imagine. Now it's time to retrieve the book cloth from its bed of boards and add the final layer of clothing to the case.

Materials

- Case with leather
- Two 7 $\frac{7}{8}$" x 11 $\frac{7}{8}$" (20cm x 30.1cm) pieces of book cloth
- Glue
- Round brush
- Bone folder
- Microspatula
- Small hammer

Instructions

1. Place one piece of book cloth wrong-side up on your work surface. Apply a thin line of glue along a long edge and make a ½" (1.3cm) fold along this edge. Run the bone folder over the fold to secure. This is the edge that will meet the leather in the groove on the case exterior. Repeat with the other book cloth.

2. Place the case exterior side up on your work surface.

3. Spread glue in a wide border along the edges of one book cloth. Spread glue in a wide border on the left side of the case.

4. Line up the folded edge of the book cloth with the edge of the leather, tucking the book cloth into the groove between the small and medium boards. Gently smooth the book cloth onto the board, working from the inside outwards and allowing even flaps to hang over the top, bottom, and left side of the case.

5. Move to the right side of the case, and spread glue in a wide border along the edges. Place the other book cloth wrong-side up on your work surface and spread glue in a wide border along the edges.

6. Lay the book cloth onto the board, tucking the folded edge into the groove and then gently smoothing the book cloth with your hands, working from the inside outwards and allowing the flaps to hang evenly over three edges of the case.

7. Turn over the case, so that the interior faces upwards. Smooth out the flaps of the book cloth at the top, bottom, and sides of the case.

8. Apply glue to the flaps on the right side of the case. Apply glue to the edges of the case that will be covered by the flaps.

9. Fold the bottom flap first, starting from the inside and working your way outwards.

10. Fold the top flap next, starting from the inside and working your way outwards.

11. Trim small triangles from the top and bottom corners of the book cloth. Use the microspatula to tuck glue into the corners, and to tuck the book cloth as you flatten the fold.

12. Fold the flap on the right side of the case, using the microspatula to tuck glue under the flap.

13. Fold over the corner.

14. Using the microspatula to tuck the fabric as smoothly as possible.

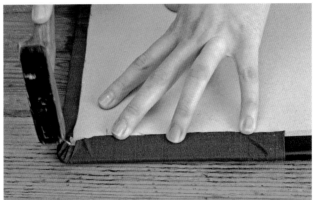

15. Tap down the top and bottom corners with the small hammer so that the book cloth lies as flat as possible on the case.

16. Repeat Steps 10 to 16 on the left side of the case.

Rounding the spine

The case is no longer bare, but it is somewhat square.
The last procedure is rounding the lightweight board that
covers the spine. This step isn't just aesthetic; a round spine
also helps keep the album stable, and prevents the book
from bulging.

1. Open the case and wrap it around a cylindrical object such as a table leg. Hold the case with both hands and gently rub back and forth around the table leg to round the spine.

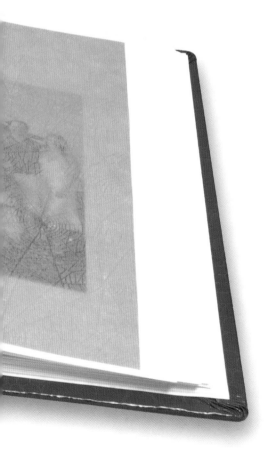

Tip

With the rhythm of a Brazilian song, we are ready for the final element in building the album: joining the block and the case.

Joining the block and the case

Connecting the two main components of the album is a simple yet critical procedure. Though the task is relatively quick, that doesn't diminish its importance. If it isn't done precisely, the whole album will be askew.

Materials

- Block
- Case with leather and book cloth
- Glue
- Round brush
- Bone folder
- Small hammer

Instructions

1. Open the case and place it interior-side up on your work surface. Place the block right-side up on your work surface.
2. Lay a piece of paper between the leaves of the front endpaper. This paper will absorb excess glue that may ooze when the block is glued to the case. If you spread your glue with a light hand, you can skip this stage.
3. Apply a thin layer of glue evenly on the top of the block.
4. Spread glue in a wide border on the binder's board that makes up the interior front cover of the case. The glue should be applied to the fabric and leather flaps, as well as the board; the center of the board should be bare.
5. Hold the block so that the spine faces the floor, and the endpaper with the glue is perpendicular to the case.
6. Allow the endpaper with the glue to open, so that it is at an angle to the cover. Bring the outer edge of the endpaper to the outer edge of the cover, ensuring that the corners are lined up and the endpaper is straight.

7. Bring the block downwards, pressing the endpaper onto the cover as you go.

8. Smooth the endpaper with your hand, starting at the edge and working towards the spine. Flatten further by running the bone folder over the endpaper, from the edge and towards the spine.

9. Close the album and strengthen the adhesion with several soft taps from the hammer.
10. Place the album on your work surface so that the back cover faces upwards. Open the cover and note where the endpaper reaches—this will give you a guide for applying glue to the back endpaper and cover.

Tip

The music that plays in my head during this process is serious and concentrated. Sometimes it is just instrumental—wind instruments primarily—of the type that declare victory after a challenging feat.

11. Lay a piece of paper between the leaves of the back endpaper. Apply a thin, even layer of glue on the back of the block.

Tip

The album is assembled. Take a break and enjoy the achievement before moving to the next stage—from the wind instruments to the cymbals—arranging the photographs!

12. Spread glue in a wide border on the binder's board that makes up the interior back cover.

13. Lift the front of the album and the block, allowing the back cover to rest on your work surface.

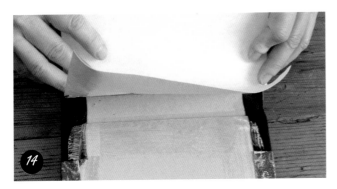

14. Grasp the corners of the endpaper with the glue and draw them towards the corners of the back cover.

15. Gently close the block, allowing the endpaper to fall onto the back cover. Guide the paper as it falls to ensure that there are no creases.

16. Smooth the endpaper with your hand, starting at the edge and working towards the spine. Flatten further with the bone folder. Tap with the hammer to smooth out any creases, and ensure the glue adheres.

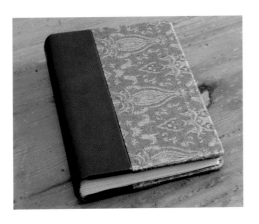

Arranging the Photographs

There is nothing quite as creative, happy, and memory-evoking as arranging photographs—the experience is particularly moving when one has constructed the album with a specific occasion in mind, as that occasion has permeated every aspect of the album. Because the album is handmade, everything is up to you: The size of the photographs. The quantity of photographs on each page. The integration of items other than photographs. You are released from the confines of store-bought albums and free to decide on the composition and layout of each and every page.

Here are some tips to help you reign in this freedom in a practical and creative manner.

Think ahead

Consider incorporating a few planned photographs in the album. This may include photographs of children holding signs (Happy Birthday Grandpa!) or photographs from a dress fitting. Though these photographs are not spontaneous, they can do wonders for creating an album whose story is really complete.

Themes

Organizing photographs by theme may seem pedantic at first, but a well-organized album pays off, as it is consistent, coherent, and pleasant to peruse. A successful album tells a story—from start to finish. It may be the story of a relationship enjoying its fortieth anniversary, a pregnancy, or a wedding. Just as stories have chapters, a photograph album has themes. Identify these themes and organize your photographs accordingly.

Collect for collages

Some photographs may not be good enough to include as-is in your album. They may have some redeeming elements, and other elements that are best forgotten. I recommend pruning these photographs to extract their best features: A gorgeous picture of the flowers. A tantalizing close-up of food. An excellent angle of a close friend. Collect the beautiful elements and assemble them in a collage based on color or theme.

Throw out bad photographs!

Even great photographers take bad photographs sometimes. Don't include these in your album. Compositions that repeat themselves, unflattering portraits, and photographs that are downright dull will simply detract from your album. Don't be sentimental! Follow your instincts and discard photographs that don't tickle your fancy.

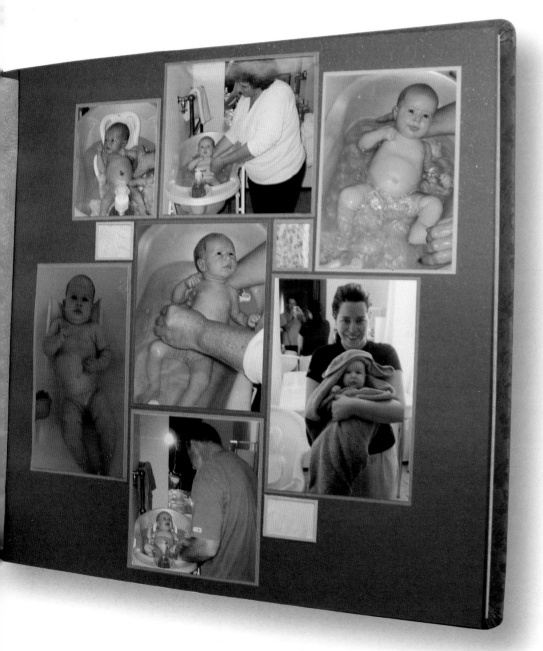

Page-by-Page Layout

Your homemade photograph album has no little plastic compartments, so you can lay out your photographs exactly as you want. Really spectacular images may merit their own page. Other photographs may share space, depending on their size and the size of the pages. Remember that you want to fill every page of the album, so arrange the pages in advance before gluing them into the album.

Affixing the photographs

You can use a variety of techniques for laying your
photographs on the page. The simplest method involves
pasting double-sided glue dots on the back of the
photograph. Add *colorful frames* by gluing the photograph
to a sheet of thin paper first. Cut straight-edged frames
using a guillotine, or add decorative frames with paper
shaper scissors. When adding paper frames, select acid-free
paper that is relatively thin. Thicker paper adds unnecessary
weight, and can cause the album to bulge. You can also add
mounting corners to some photographs, although I
recommend pasting the photographs first with glue dots.
Mounting corners are an excellent way of setting off really
spectacular photographs that merit their own page.

Also Available From
Creative Publishing International

To purchase
these or other
Creative Publishing
International titles,
contact your local
bookseller, or visit
our website at
www.creativepub.com

Designer Bead Embroidery
150 Patterns and Complete Techniques
by Kenneth D. King

Wreaths and Wallflowers
Gorgeous Decorations with Silk and
Dried Florals
By Ardith Beveridge

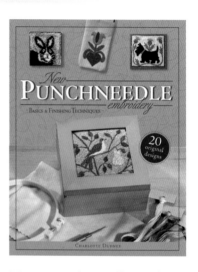

New Punchneedle Embroidery
Basics & Finishing Techniques
by Charlotte Dudney

Embellished Appliqué
20 Machine-Stitched Projects for Fashion
Items and Personal Gifts
by Patricia Converse

50 Ways to Paint Furniture
The Easy Step-by-Step Way to Decorator Looks
By Elise C. Kinkead